MESSAGES
FROM THE
Mermaids
COLOURING BOOK

MESSAGES
FROM THE

Mermaids
COLOURING BOOK

DOREEN VIRTUE

Illustrations by Norma J. Burnell

HAY HOUSE

Carlsbad, California • New York City • London
Sydney •Johannesburg • Vancouver • New Delhi

First published and distributed in the United Kingdom by:
Hay House UK Ltd, Astley House, 33 Notting Hill Gate, London W11 3JQ
Tel: +44 (0)20 3675 2450; Fax: +44 (0)20 3675 2451; www.hayhouse.co.uk

Published and distributed in the United States of America by:
Hay House Inc., PO Box 5100, Carlsbad, CA 92018-5100
Tel: (1) 760 431 7695 or (800) 654 5126
Fax: (1) 760 431 6948 or (800) 650 5115; www.hayhouse.com

Published and distributed in Australia by:
Hay House Australia Ltd, 18/36 Ralph St, Alexandria NSW 2015
Tel: (61) 2 9669 4299; Fax: (61) 2 9669 4144; www.hayhouse.com.au

Published and distributed in the Republic of South Africa by:
Hay House SA (Pty) Ltd, PO Box 990, Witkoppen 2068
info@hayhouse.co.za; www.hayhouse.co.za

Published and distributed in India by:
Hay House Publishers India, Muskaan Complex, Plot No.3, B-2,
Vasant Kunj, New Delhi 110 070
Tel: (91) 11 4176 1620; Fax: (91) 11 4176 1630; www.hayhouse.co.in

Distributed in Canada by:
Raincoast Books, 2440 Viking Way, Richmond, B.C. V6V 1N2
Tel: (1) 604 448 7100; Fax: (1) 604 270 7161; www.raincoast.com

A catalogue record for this book is available from the British Library.

ISBN: 978-1-78180-926-6

Printed and bound by CPI Group (UK) Ltd, Croydon, CR0 4YY

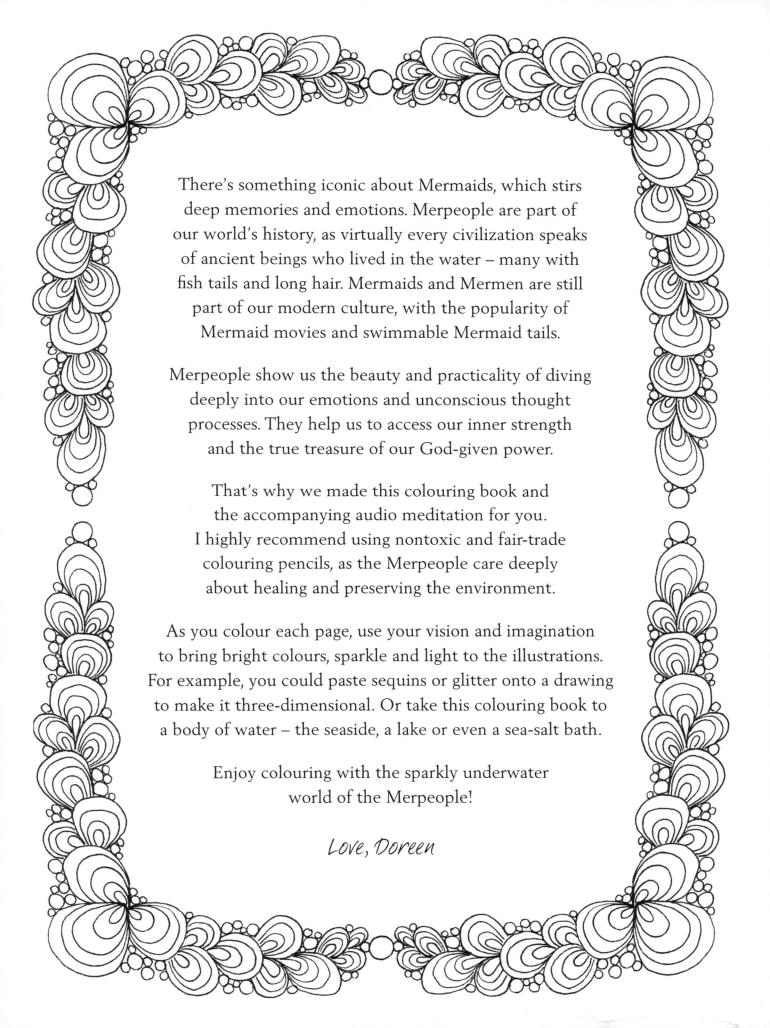

There's something iconic about Mermaids, which stirs
deep memories and emotions. Merpeople are part of
our world's history, as virtually every civilization speaks
of ancient beings who lived in the water – many with
fish tails and long hair. Mermaids and Mermen are still
part of our modern culture, with the popularity of
Mermaid movies and swimmable Mermaid tails.

Merpeople show us the beauty and practicality of diving
deeply into our emotions and unconscious thought
processes. They help us to access our inner strength
and the true treasure of our God-given power.

That's why we made this colouring book and
the accompanying audio meditation for you.
I highly recommend using nontoxic and fair-trade
colouring pencils, as the Merpeople care deeply
about healing and preserving the environment.

As you colour each page, use your vision and imagination
to bring bright colours, sparkle and light to the illustrations.
For example, you could paste sequins or glitter onto a drawing
to make it three-dimensional. Or take this colouring book to
a body of water – the seaside, a lake or even a sea-salt bath.

Enjoy colouring with the sparkly underwater
world of the Merpeople!

Love, Doreen

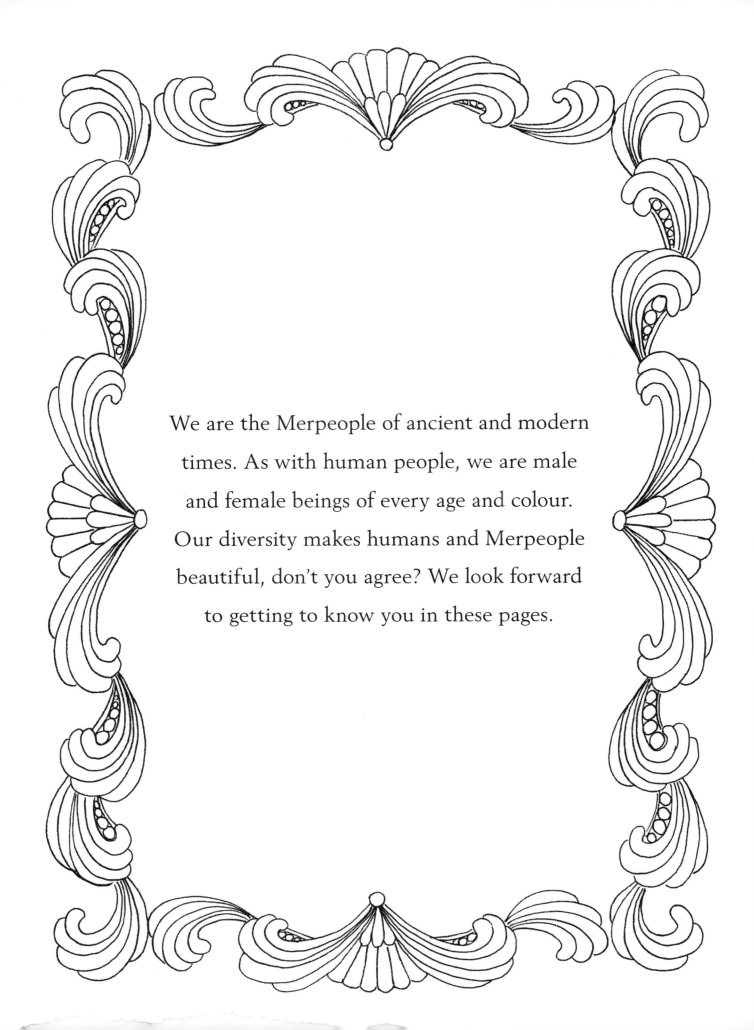

We are the Merpeople of ancient and modern times. As with human people, we are male and female beings of every age and colour. Our diversity makes humans and Merpeople beautiful, don't you agree? We look forward to getting to know you in these pages.

We are the guardians of the waters,
ensuring that they're respected and
protected. You can work with us to
help keep the waters safe and pure by
choosing ecofriendly cleaning supplies.
That way, what you rinse down the drain
is friendly to the fish and the reefs.

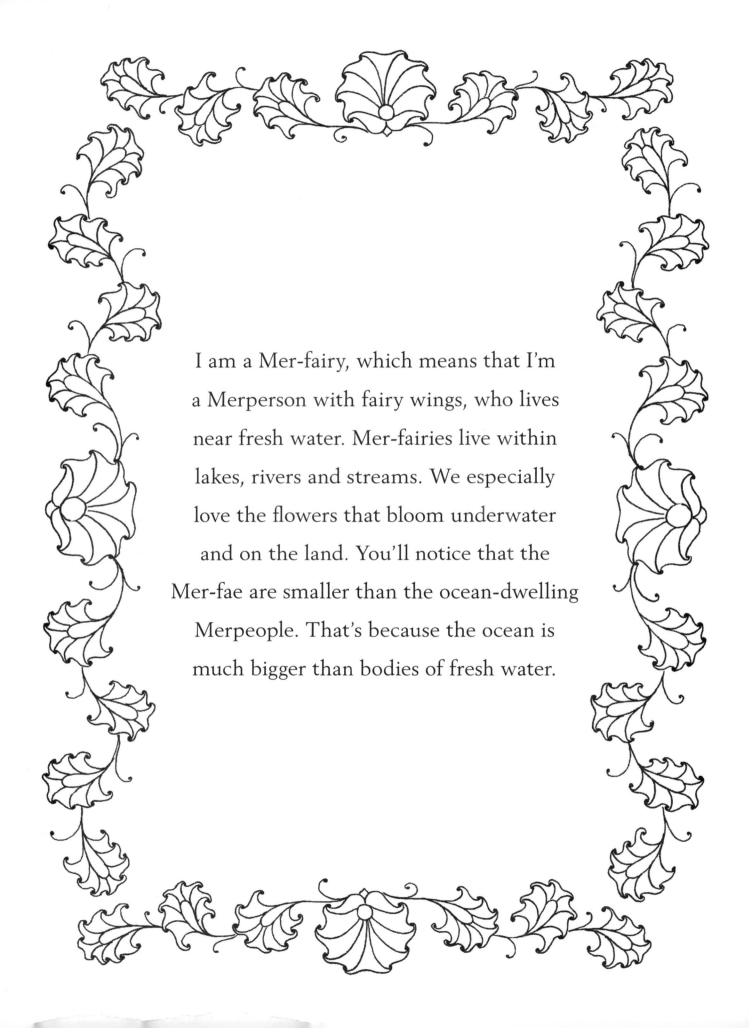

I am a Mer-fairy, which means that I'm a Merperson with fairy wings, who lives near fresh water. Mer-fairies live within lakes, rivers and streams. We especially love the flowers that bloom underwater and on the land. You'll notice that the Mer-fae are smaller than the ocean-dwelling Merpeople. That's because the ocean is much bigger than bodies of fresh water.

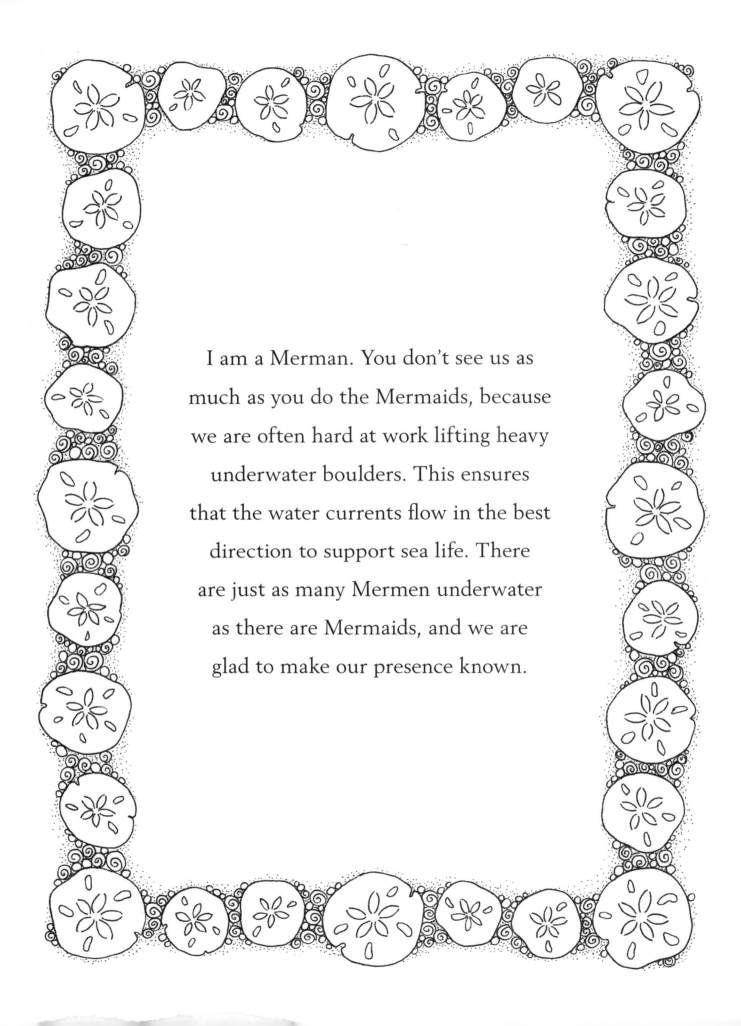

I am a Merman. You don't see us as much as you do the Mermaids, because we are often hard at work lifting heavy underwater boulders. This ensures that the water currents flow in the best direction to support sea life. There are just as many Mermen underwater as there are Mermaids, and we are glad to make our presence known.

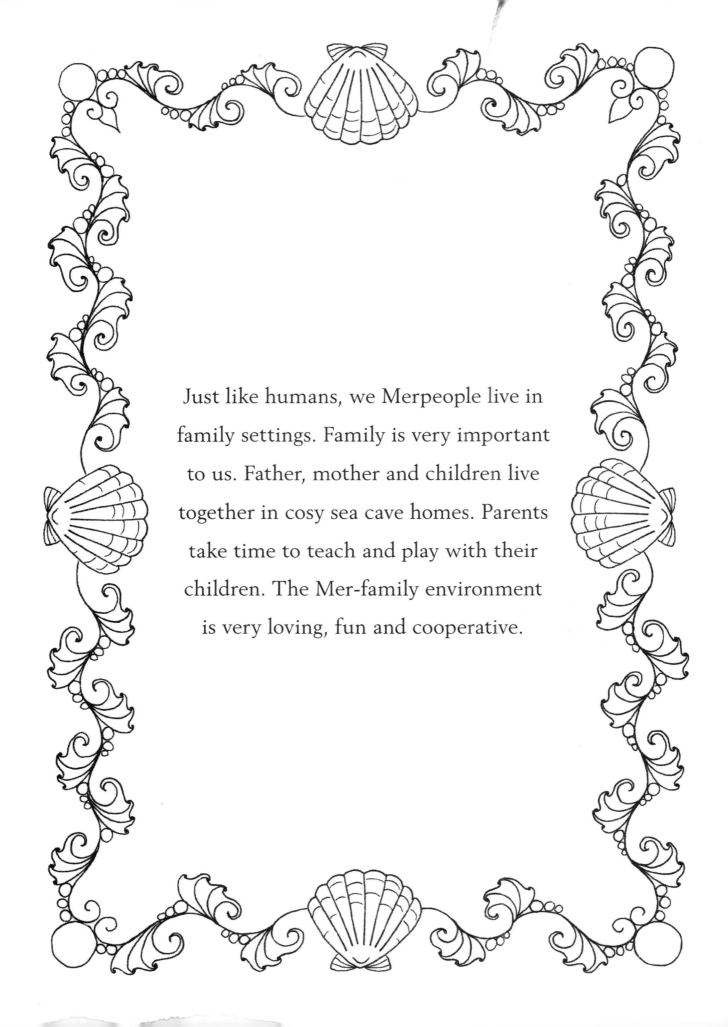

Just like humans, we Merpeople live in family settings. Family is very important to us. Father, mother and children live together in cosy sea cave homes. Parents take time to teach and play with their children. The Mer-family environment is very loving, fun and cooperative.

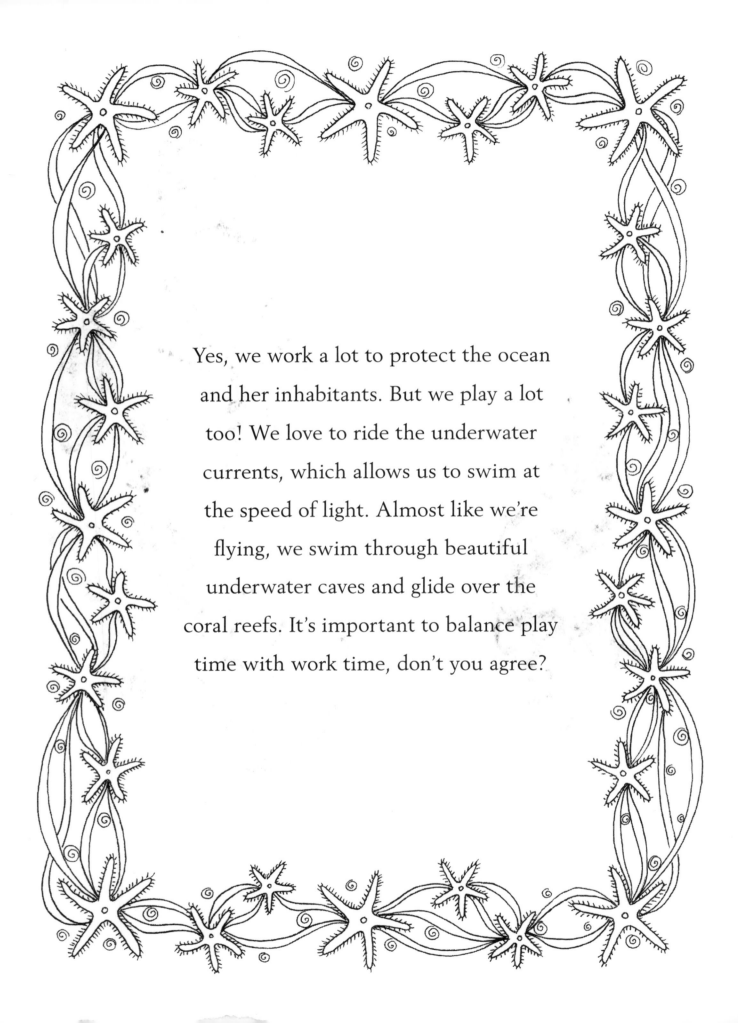

Yes, we work a lot to protect the ocean and her inhabitants. But we play a lot too! We love to ride the underwater currents, which allows us to swim at the speed of light. Almost like we're flying, we swim through beautiful underwater caves and glide over the coral reefs. It's important to balance play time with work time, don't you agree?

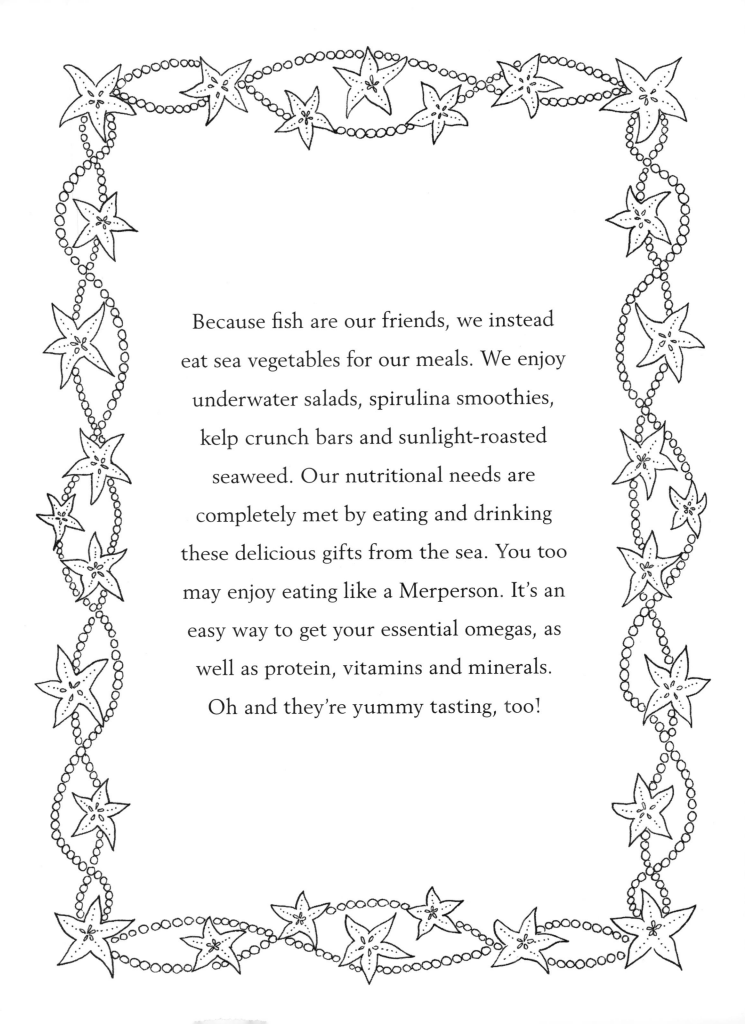

Because fish are our friends, we instead eat sea vegetables for our meals. We enjoy underwater salads, spirulina smoothies, kelp crunch bars and sunlight-roasted seaweed. Our nutritional needs are completely met by eating and drinking these delicious gifts from the sea. You too may enjoy eating like a Merperson. It's an easy way to get your essential omegas, as well as protein, vitamins and minerals. Oh and they're yummy tasting, too!

You can connect with us Merpeople whenever you visit the ocean or a lake. We're always excited to meet people who are environmentally conscious. So if you help us to protect the waters, we'll become instant friends. For example, picking up litter that's next to the water will ensure that it doesn't fall in and accidentally be swallowed by fish or other water dwellers.

We love fish – not to eat, but as our friends and companions. The next time you're swimming in the ocean or a lake, listen carefully and you'll hear the symphony of music that the fishes create! We all communicate melodically. If you do eat fish, we hope that you'll choose a sustainable (not endangered) fish and definitely not factory-farmed fish. We all deserve to be free and wild!

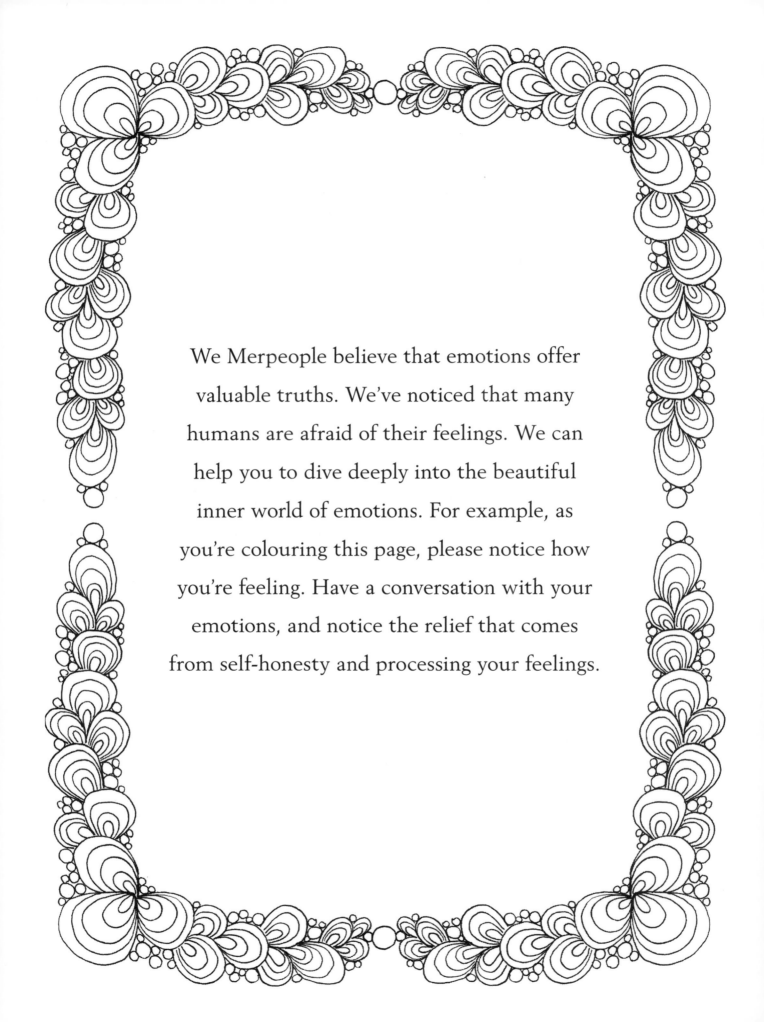

We Merpeople believe that emotions offer valuable truths. We've noticed that many humans are afraid of their feelings. We can help you to dive deeply into the beautiful inner world of emotions. For example, as you're colouring this page, please notice how you're feeling. Have a conversation with your emotions, and notice the relief that comes from self-honesty and processing your feelings.

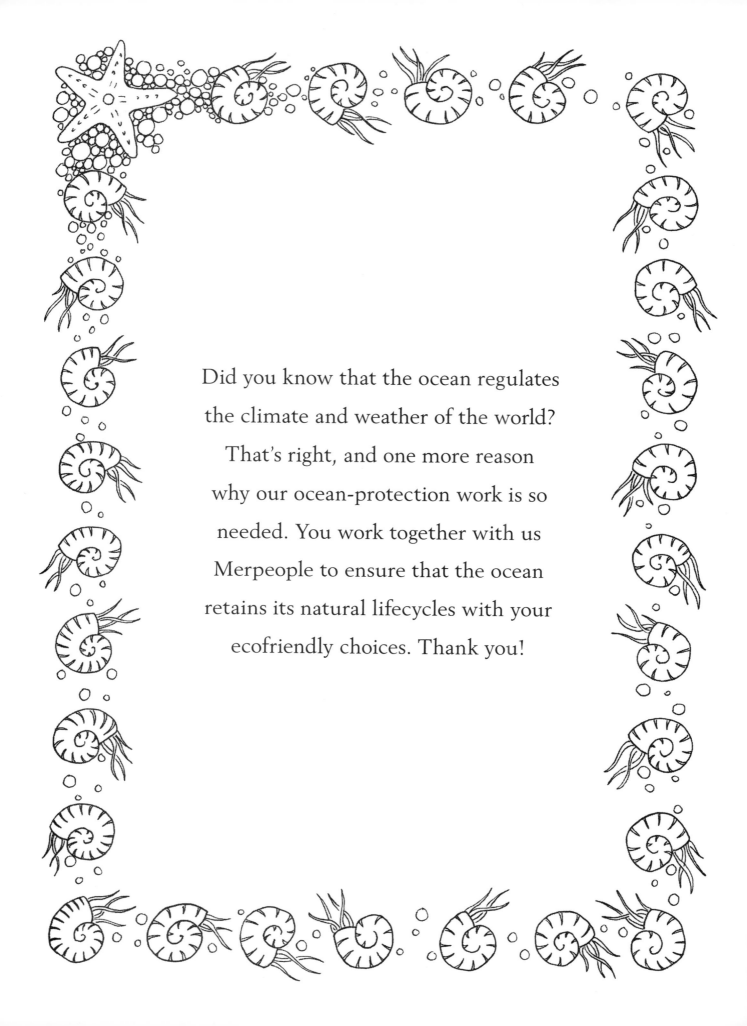

Did you know that the ocean regulates
the climate and weather of the world?
That's right, and one more reason
why our ocean-protection work is so
needed. You work together with us
Merpeople to ensure that the ocean
retains its natural lifecycles with your
ecofriendly choices. Thank you!

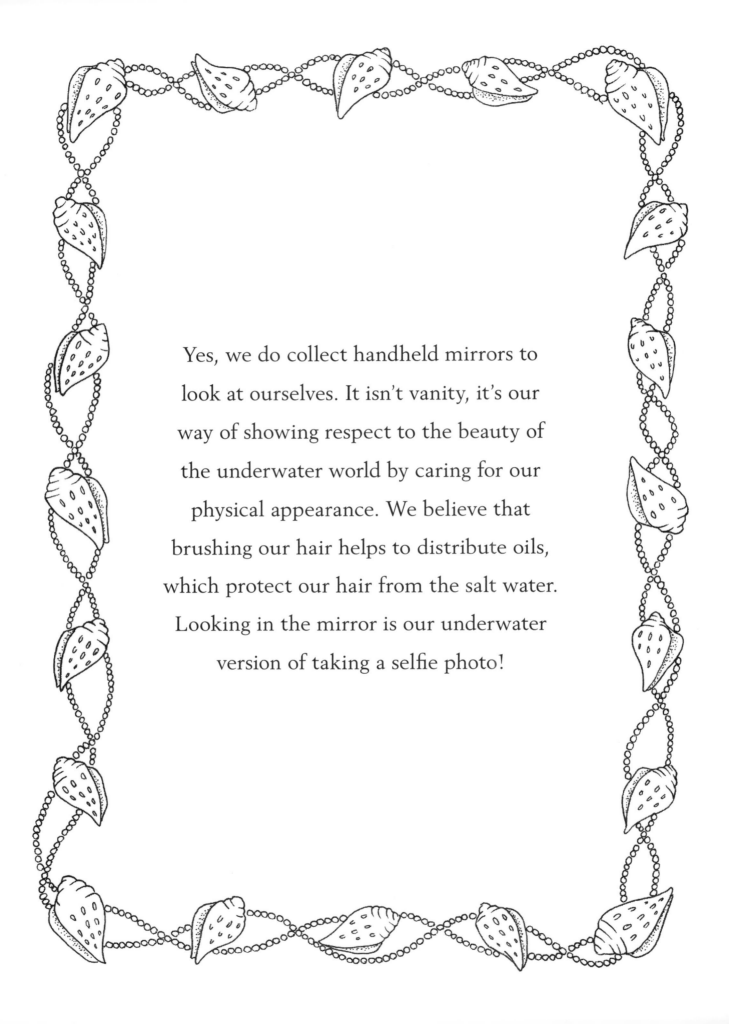

Yes, we do collect handheld mirrors to look at ourselves. It isn't vanity, it's our way of showing respect to the beauty of the underwater world by caring for our physical appearance. We believe that brushing our hair helps to distribute oils, which protect our hair from the salt water. Looking in the mirror is our underwater version of taking a selfie photo!

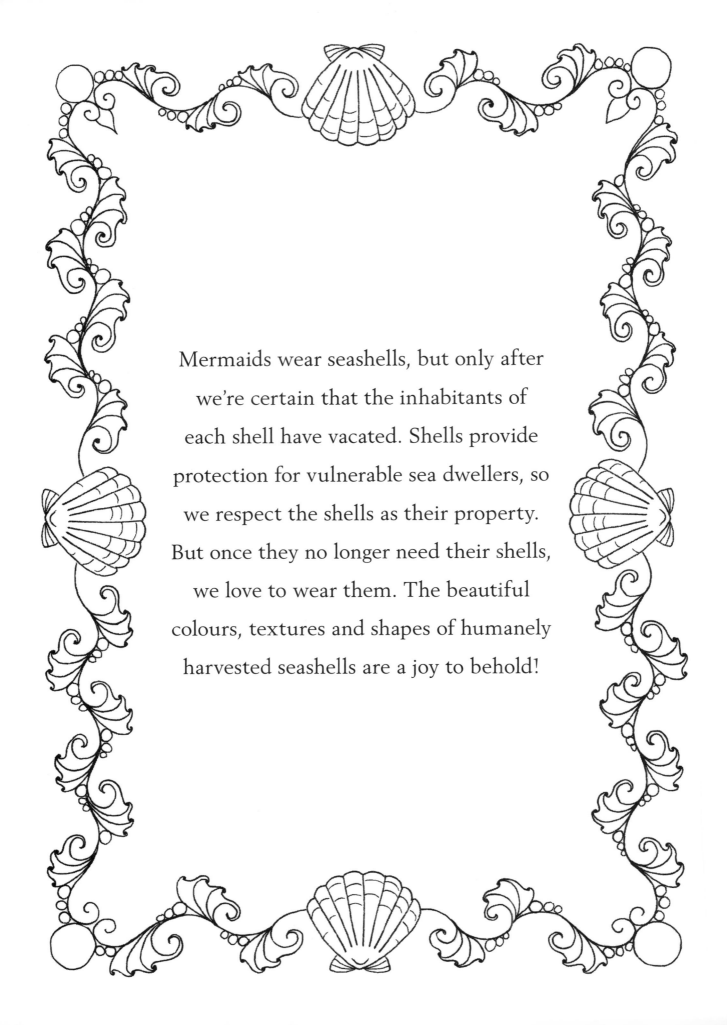

Mermaids wear seashells, but only after we're certain that the inhabitants of each shell have vacated. Shells provide protection for vulnerable sea dwellers, so we respect the shells as their property. But once they no longer need their shells, we love to wear them. The beautiful colours, textures and shapes of humanely harvested seashells are a joy to behold!

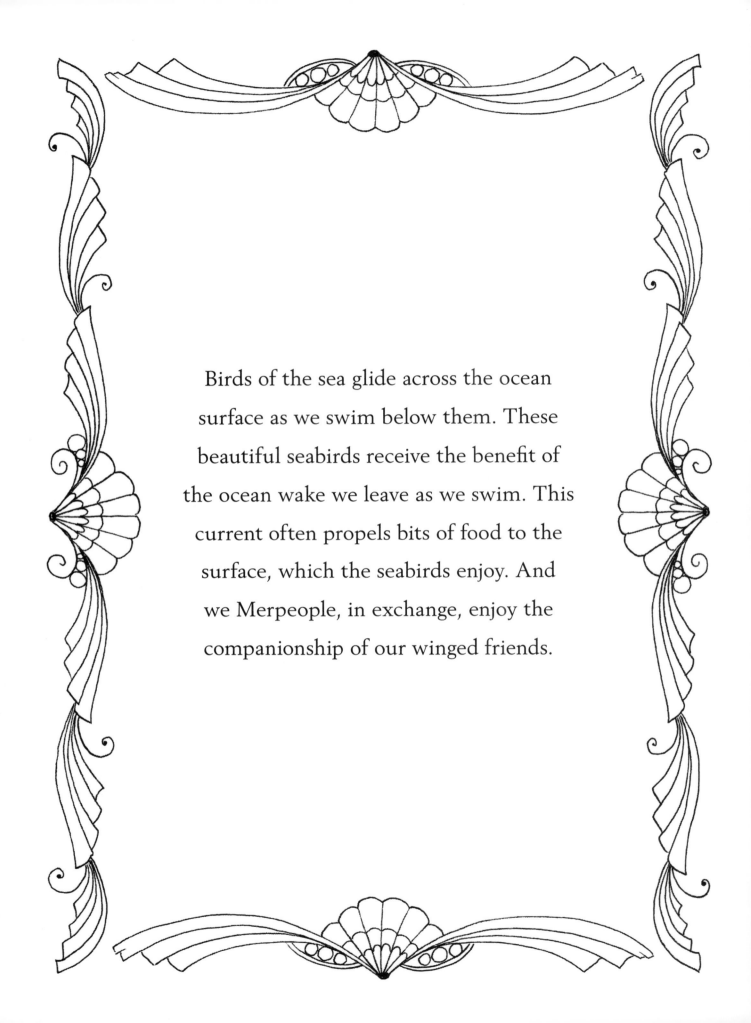

Birds of the sea glide across the ocean surface as we swim below them. These beautiful seabirds receive the benefit of the ocean wake we leave as we swim. This current often propels bits of food to the surface, which the seabirds enjoy. And we Merpeople, in exchange, enjoy the companionship of our winged friends.

Most of the time, we Merpeople live and work together in a family and community environment. Yet we all need alone-time to rest and reflect upon our feelings. So, each of us goes on retreat. First though, we tell our Mer-family members of our plans and destination, as a safety measure and courtesy. After all, clear communication is an action of love.

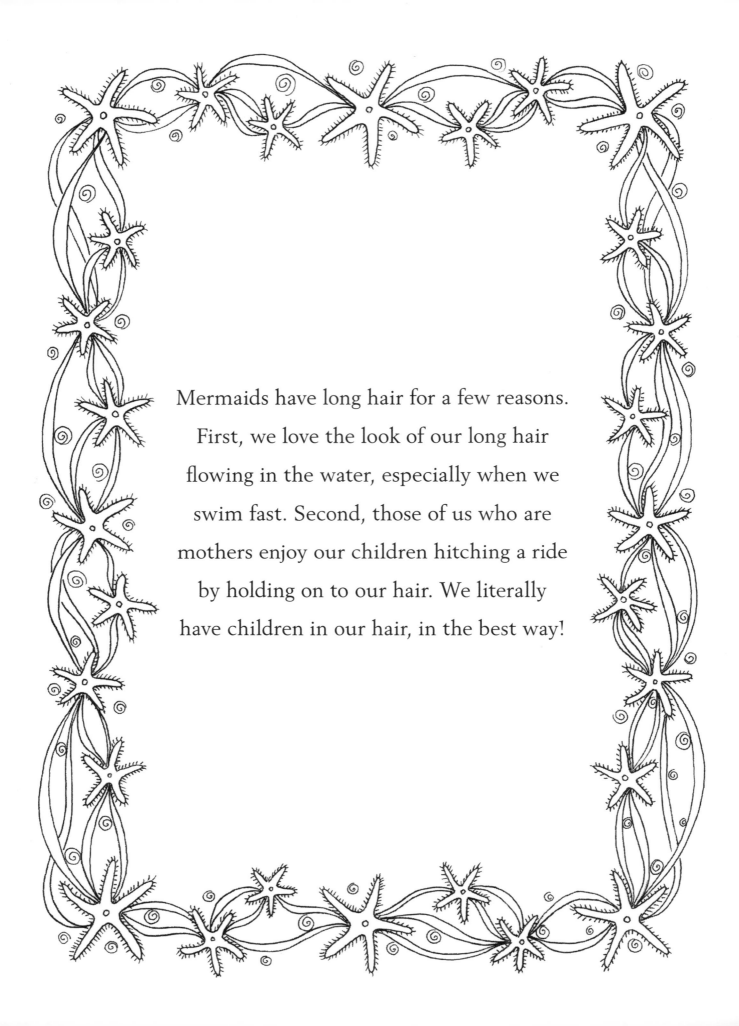

Mermaids have long hair for a few reasons. First, we love the look of our long hair flowing in the water, especially when we swim fast. Second, those of us who are mothers enjoy our children hitching a ride by holding on to our hair. We literally have children in our hair, in the best way!

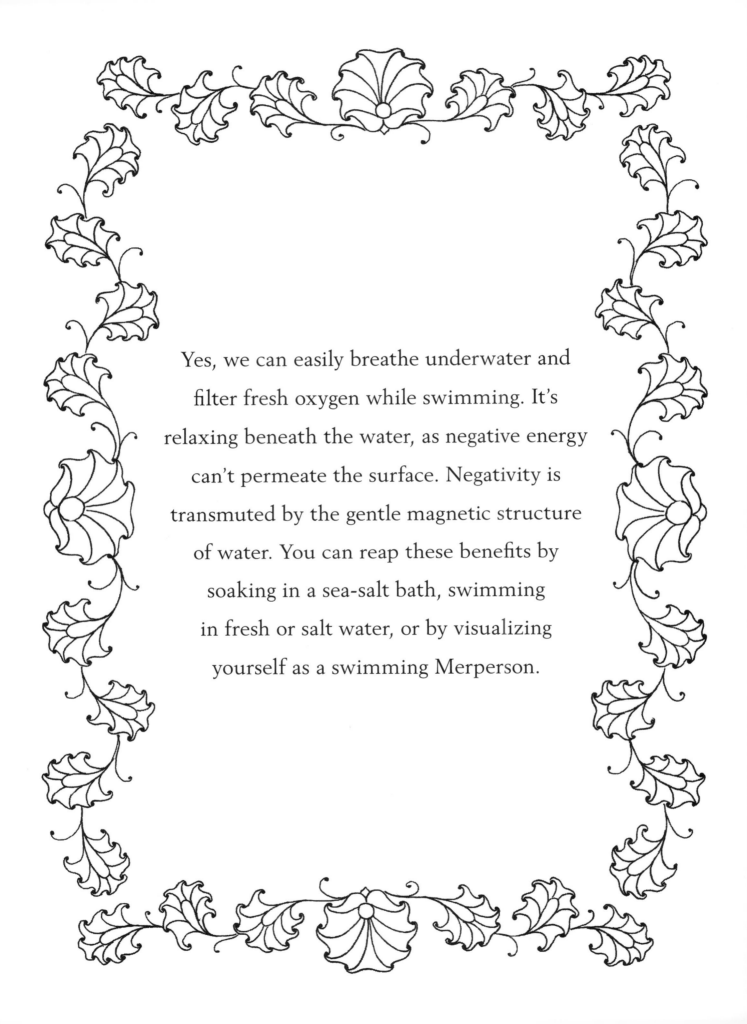

Yes, we can easily breathe underwater and filter fresh oxygen while swimming. It's relaxing beneath the water, as negative energy can't permeate the surface. Negativity is transmuted by the gentle magnetic structure of water. You can reap these benefits by soaking in a sea-salt bath, swimming in fresh or salt water, or by visualizing yourself as a swimming Merperson.

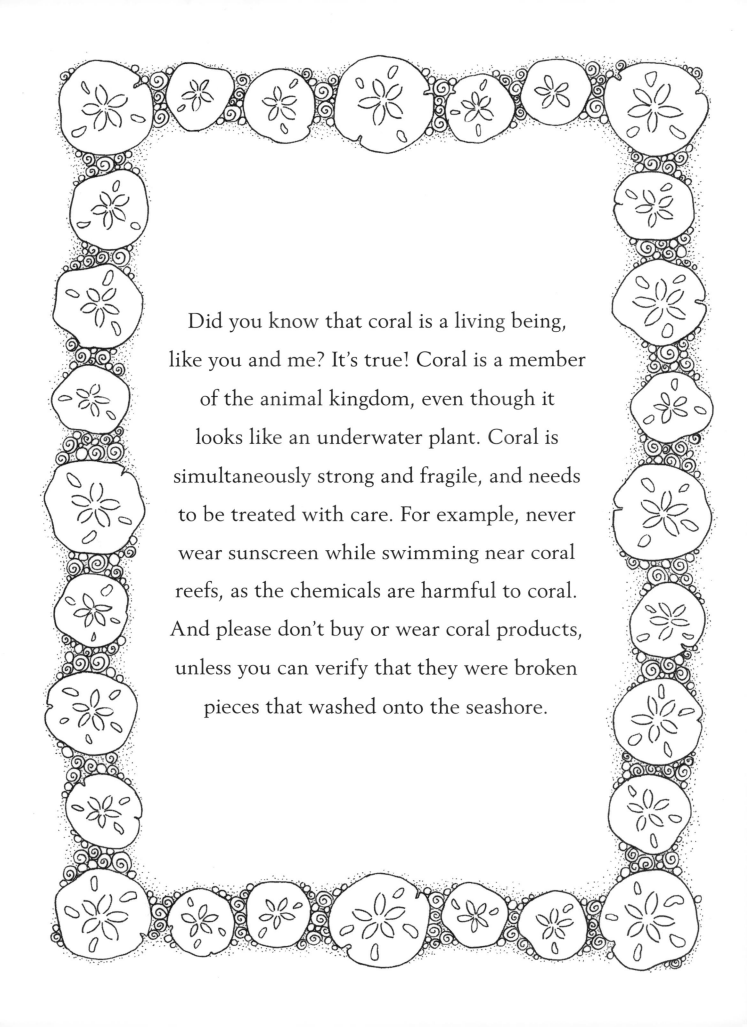

Did you know that coral is a living being, like you and me? It's true! Coral is a member of the animal kingdom, even though it looks like an underwater plant. Coral is simultaneously strong and fragile, and needs to be treated with care. For example, never wear sunscreen while swimming near coral reefs, as the chemicals are harmful to coral. And please don't buy or wear coral products, unless you can verify that they were broken pieces that washed onto the seashore.

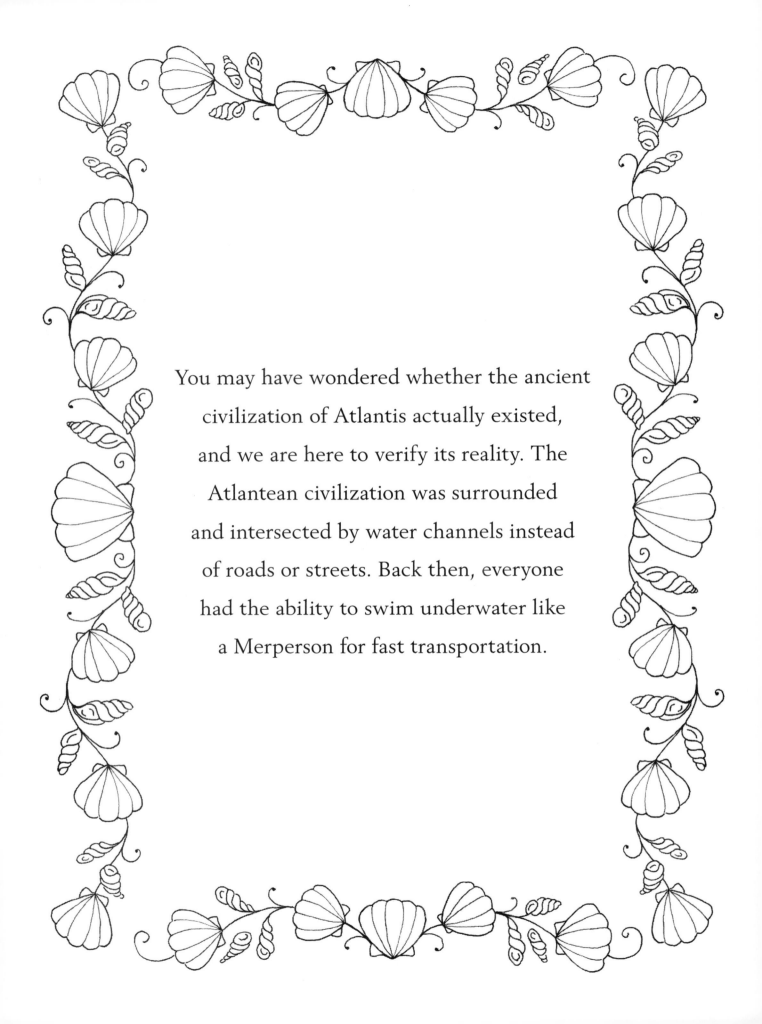

You may have wondered whether the ancient civilization of Atlantis actually existed, and we are here to verify its reality. The Atlantean civilization was surrounded and intersected by water channels instead of roads or streets. Back then, everyone had the ability to swim underwater like a Merperson for fast transportation.

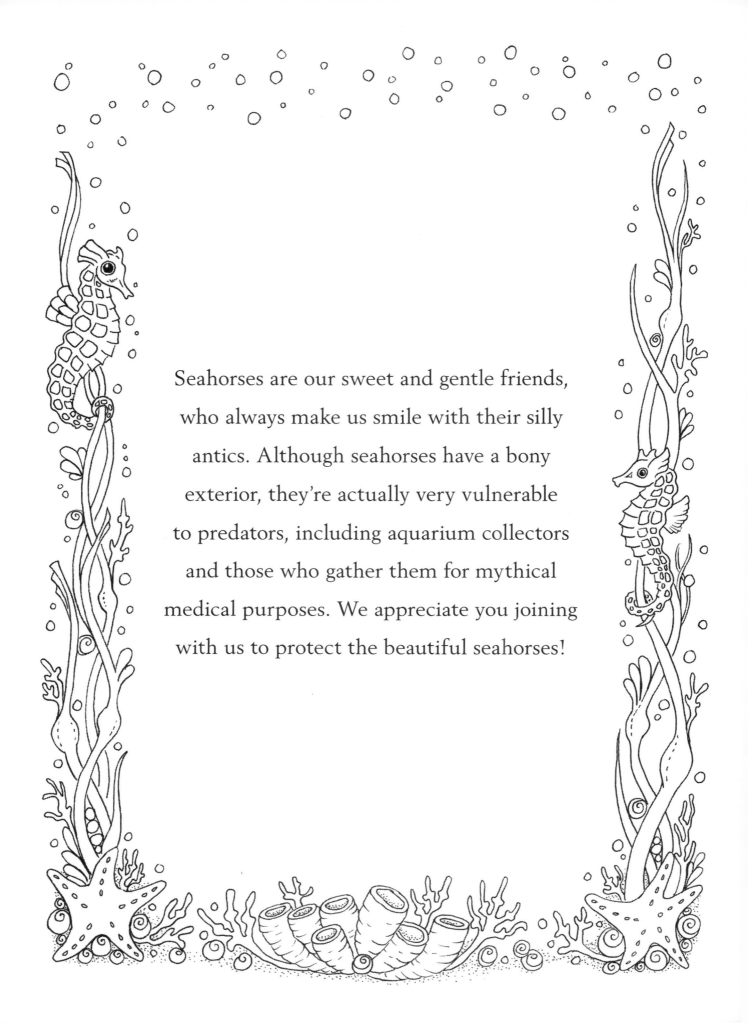

Seahorses are our sweet and gentle friends, who always make us smile with their silly antics. Although seahorses have a bony exterior, they're actually very vulnerable to predators, including aquarium collectors and those who gather them for mythical medical purposes. We appreciate you joining with us to protect the beautiful seahorses!

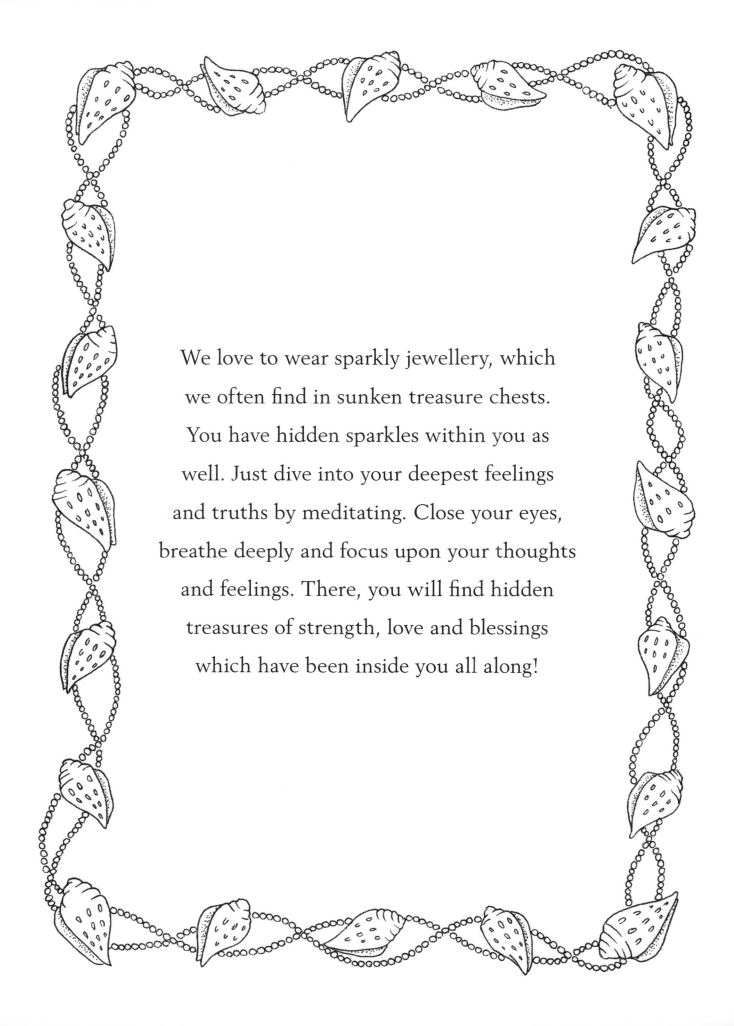

We love to wear sparkly jewellery, which
we often find in sunken treasure chests.
You have hidden sparkles within you as
well. Just dive into your deepest feelings
and truths by meditating. Close your eyes,
breathe deeply and focus upon your thoughts
and feelings. There, you will find hidden
treasures of strength, love and blessings
which have been inside you all along!

Everyone has a beautiful singing voice, but you may not appreciate your own melodies unless you try! Practise singing around water, such as in the shower or bath, or even at the seashore, to build your confidence and appreciation of your voice. Water amplifies the emotional connection with music. We've also discovered that singing leads to a more melodic speaking voice, which inspires others to listen to you. Just pretend your hairbrush is a microphone, and sing from your soul!

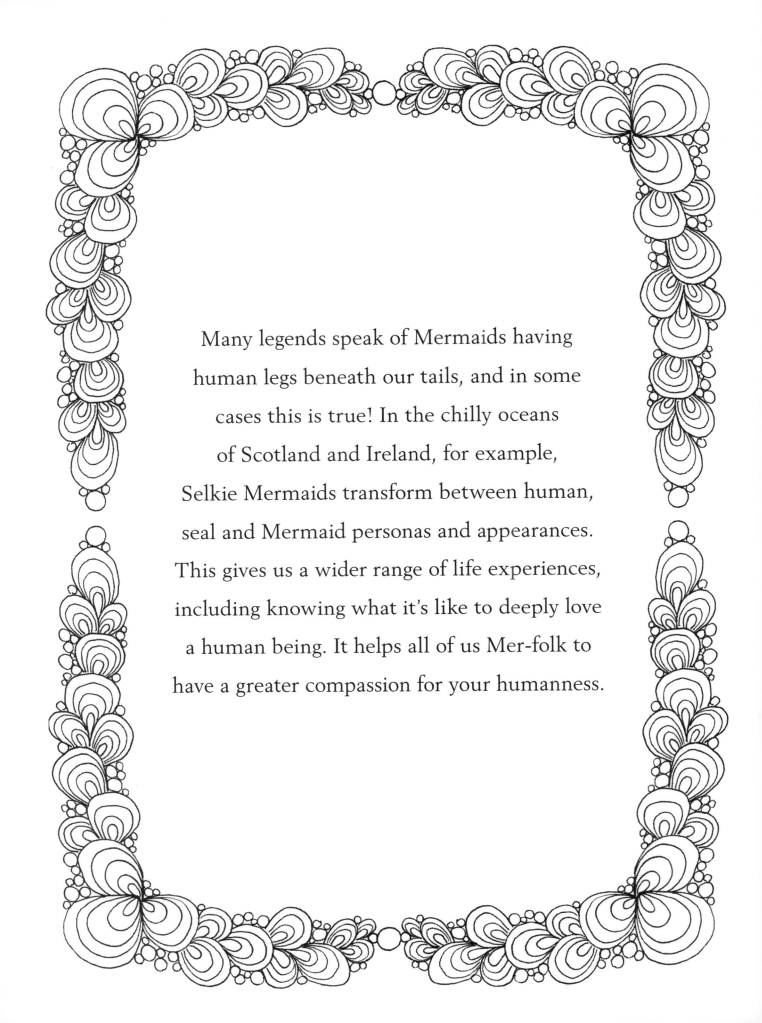

Many legends speak of Mermaids having human legs beneath our tails, and in some cases this is true! In the chilly oceans of Scotland and Ireland, for example, Selkie Mermaids transform between human, seal and Mermaid personas and appearances. This gives us a wider range of life experiences, including knowing what it's like to deeply love a human being. It helps all of us Mer-folk to have a greater compassion for your humanness.

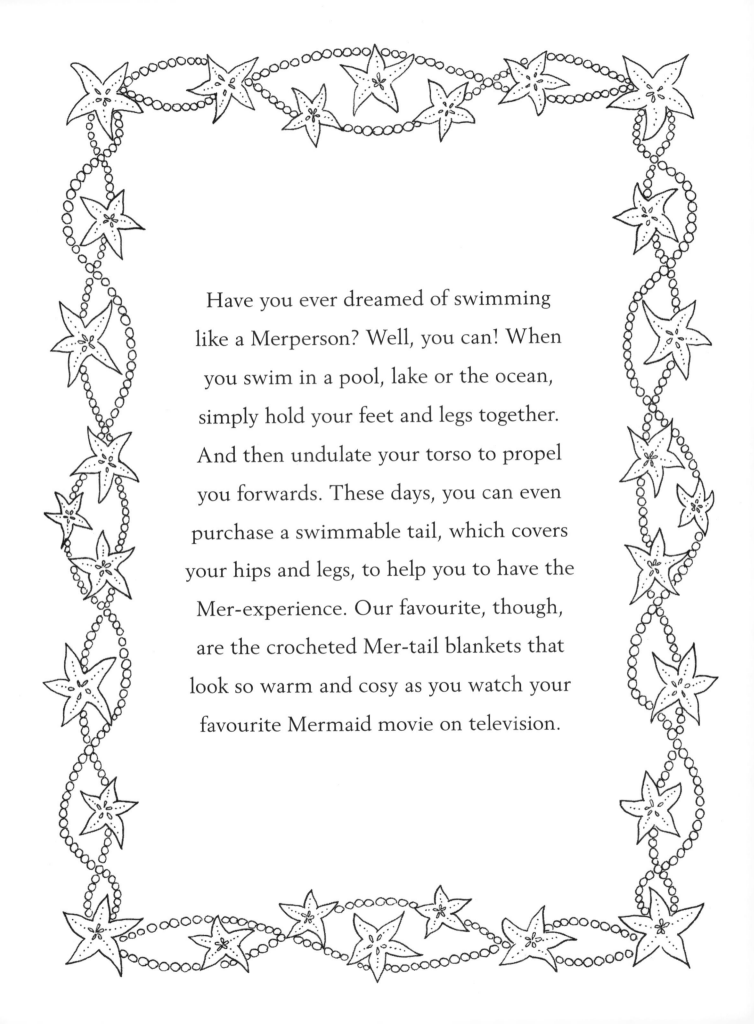

Have you ever dreamed of swimming like a Merperson? Well, you can! When you swim in a pool, lake or the ocean, simply hold your feet and legs together. And then undulate your torso to propel you forwards. These days, you can even purchase a swimmable tail, which covers your hips and legs, to help you to have the Mer-experience. Our favourite, though, are the crocheted Mer-tail blankets that look so warm and cosy as you watch your favourite Mermaid movie on television.

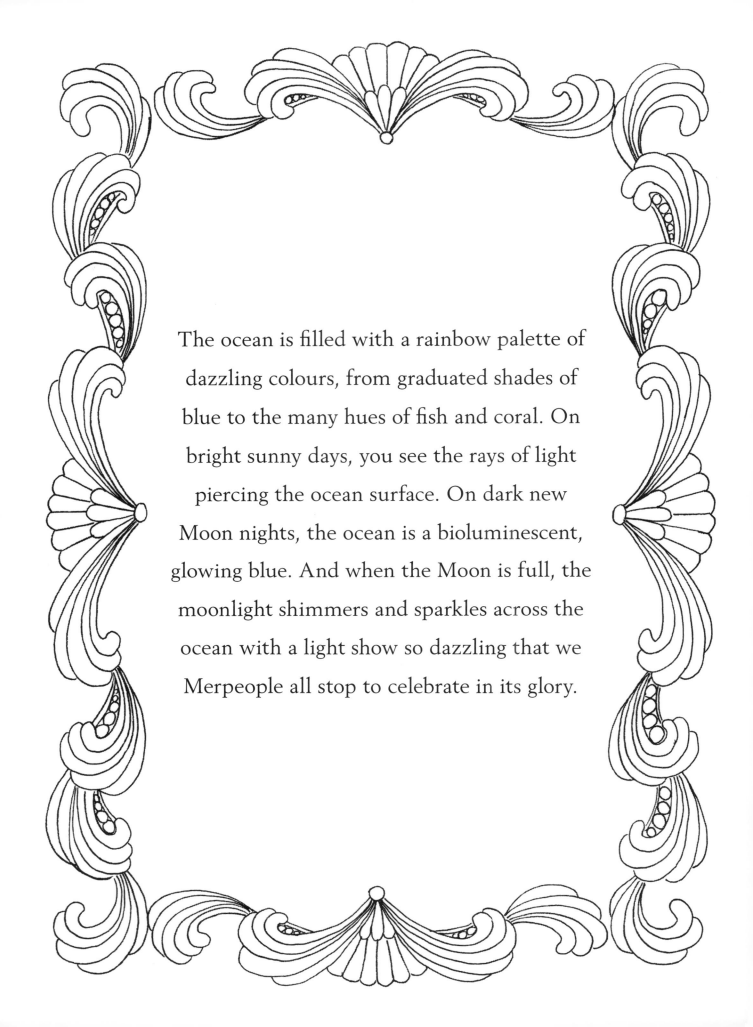

The ocean is filled with a rainbow palette of dazzling colours, from graduated shades of blue to the many hues of fish and coral. On bright sunny days, you see the rays of light piercing the ocean surface. On dark new Moon nights, the ocean is a bioluminescent, glowing blue. And when the Moon is full, the moonlight shimmers and sparkles across the ocean with a light show so dazzling that we Merpeople all stop to celebrate in its glory.

Since ancient times, humans have been aware of our presence. Statues of we Merpeople can be found in virtually every civilization. We aren't looking for special recognition, we're just celebrating our long history together on Earth. Wherever there's water, you'll find us in modern and ancient times!

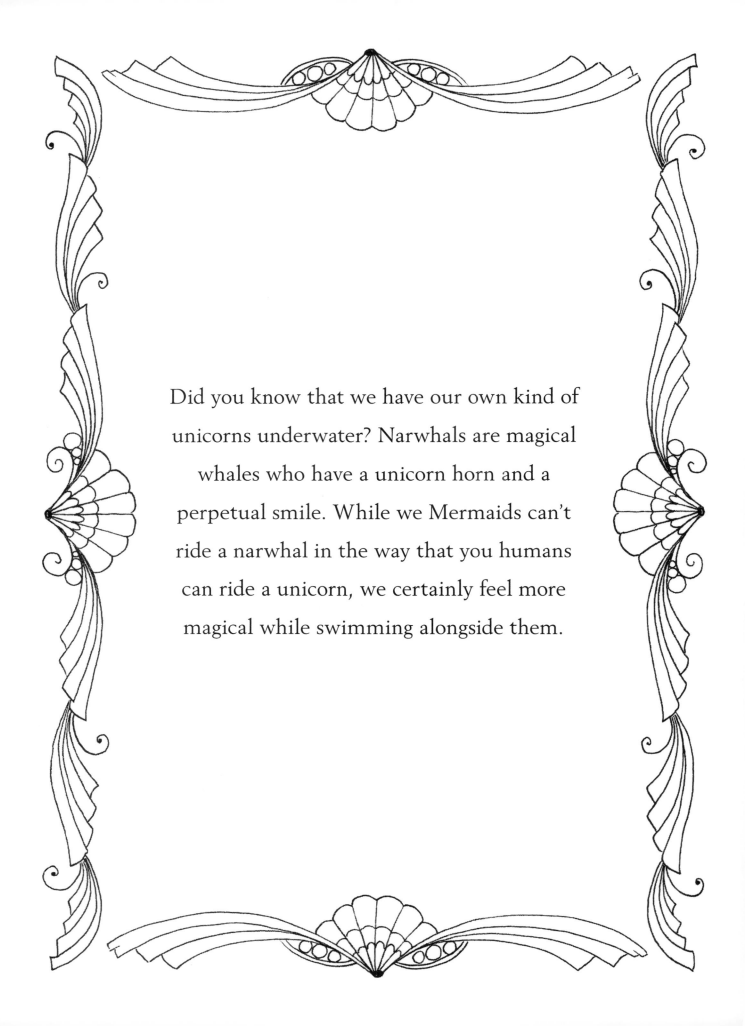

Did you know that we have our own kind of unicorns underwater? Narwhals are magical whales who have a unicorn horn and a perpetual smile. While we Mermaids can't ride a narwhal in the way that you humans can ride a unicorn, we certainly feel more magical while swimming alongside them.

Dolphins are our cousins, and we share so much in common! Dolphins have their own unique language, which you can hear and understand in your heart. When we get too serious about life, a pod of dolphins will swim by to remind us that we can accomplish our responsibilities while being playful and having fun along the way!

Just as dolphins remind us to incorporate playfulness into our daily duties, so do sea turtles remind us to swim a bit slower so that we can enjoy the scenery. Sea turtles love to float in the ocean while tiny fish clean algae from their shells. This is their demonstration that self-care often involves stopping what you're doing, relaxing and allowing others to help you.

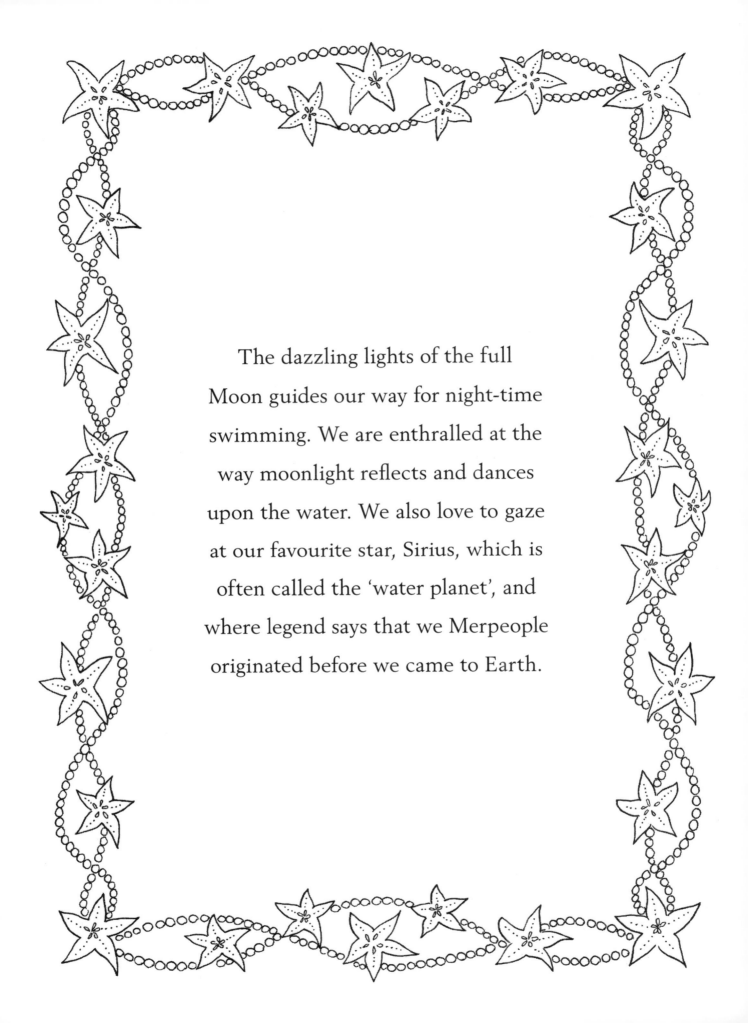

The dazzling lights of the full
Moon guides our way for night-time
swimming. We are enthralled at the
way moonlight reflects and dances
upon the water. We also love to gaze
at our favourite star, Sirius, which is
often called the 'water planet', and
where legend says that we Merpeople
originated before we came to Earth.

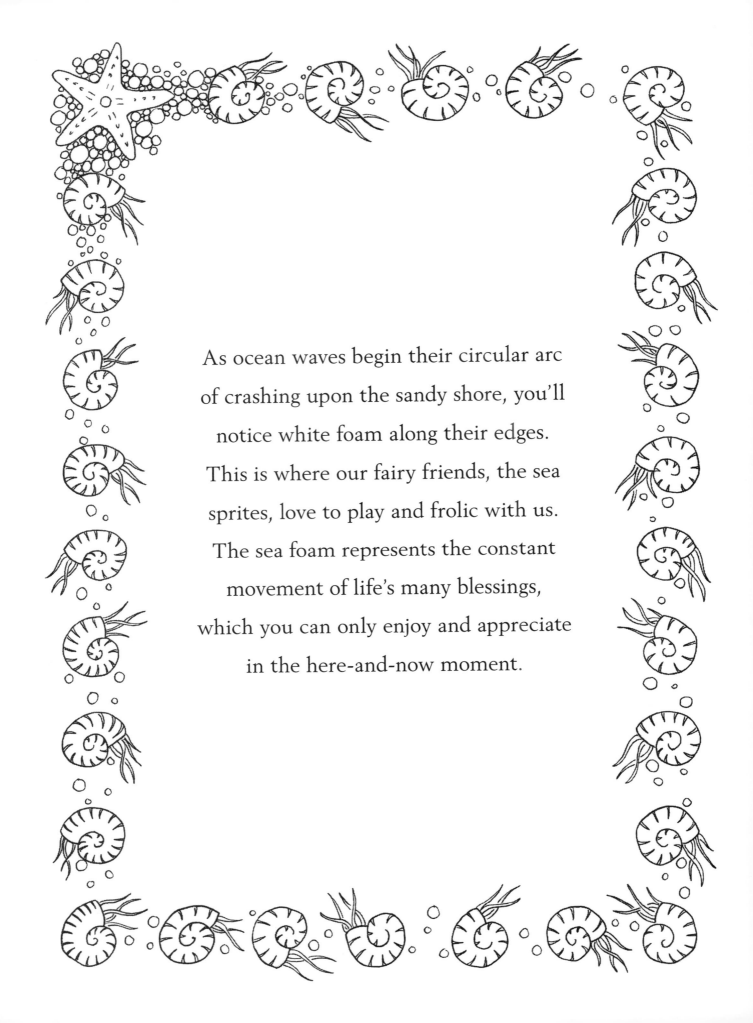

As ocean waves begin their circular arc
of crashing upon the sandy shore, you'll
notice white foam along their edges.
This is where our fairy friends, the sea
sprites, love to play and frolic with us.
The sea foam represents the constant
movement of life's many blessings,
which you can only enjoy and appreciate
in the here-and-now moment.

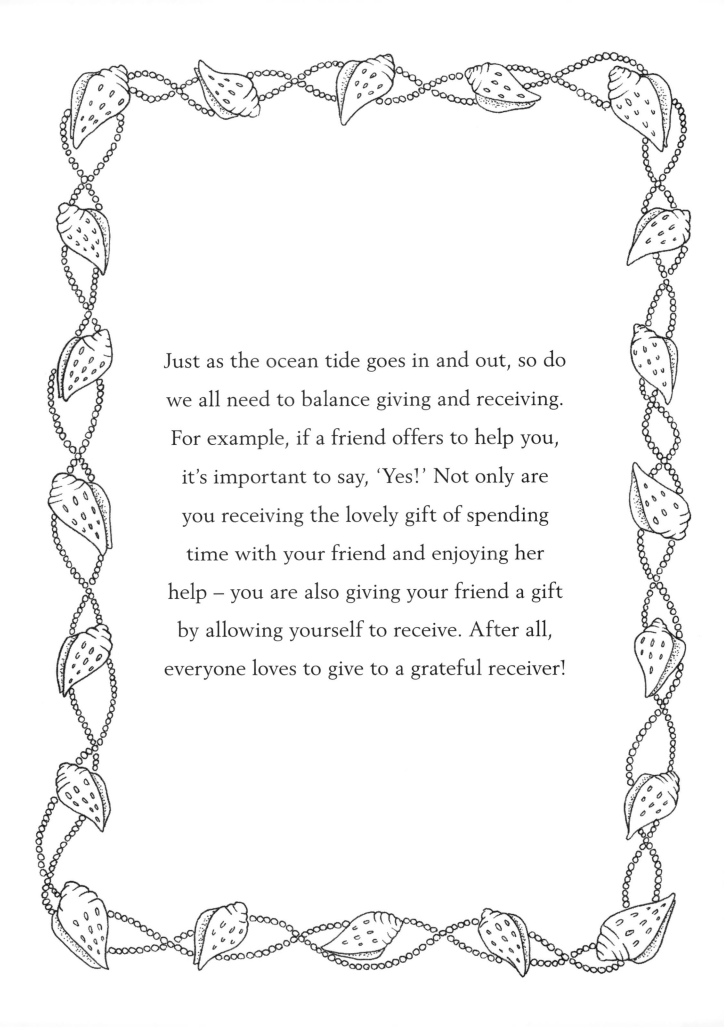

Just as the ocean tide goes in and out, so do
we all need to balance giving and receiving.
For example, if a friend offers to help you,
it's important to say, 'Yes!' Not only are
you receiving the lovely gift of spending
time with your friend and enjoying her
help – you are also giving your friend a gift
by allowing yourself to receive. After all,
everyone loves to give to a grateful receiver!

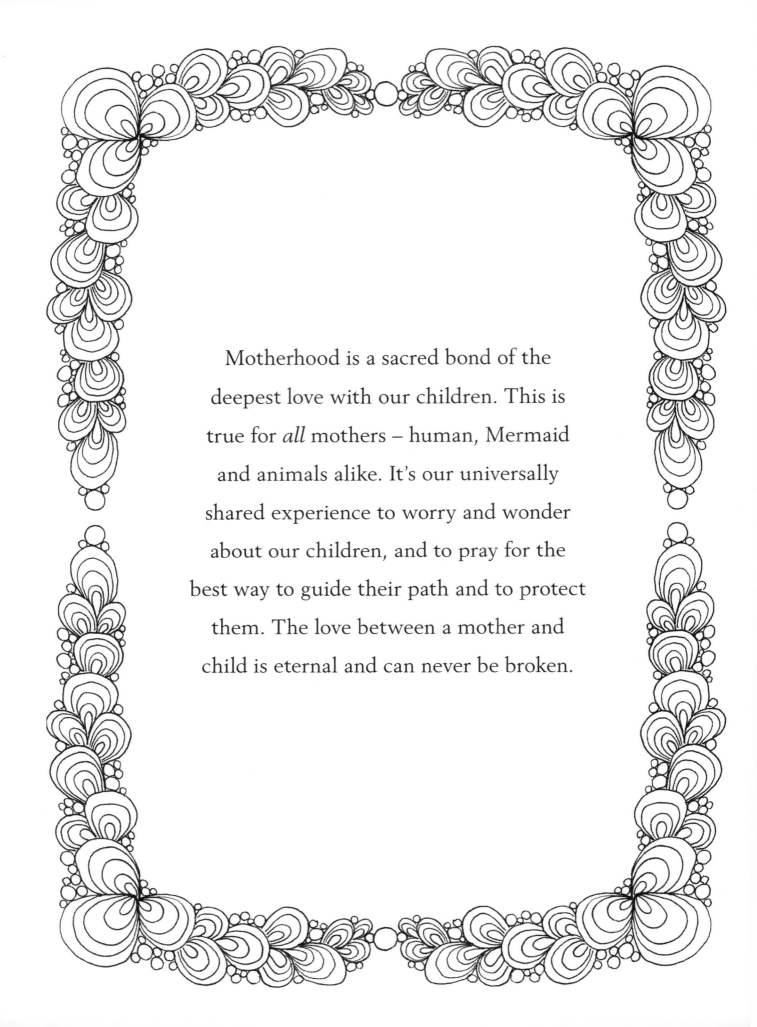

Motherhood is a sacred bond of the deepest love with our children. This is true for *all* mothers – human, Mermaid and animals alike. It's our universally shared experience to worry and wonder about our children, and to pray for the best way to guide their path and to protect them. The love between a mother and child is eternal and can never be broken.

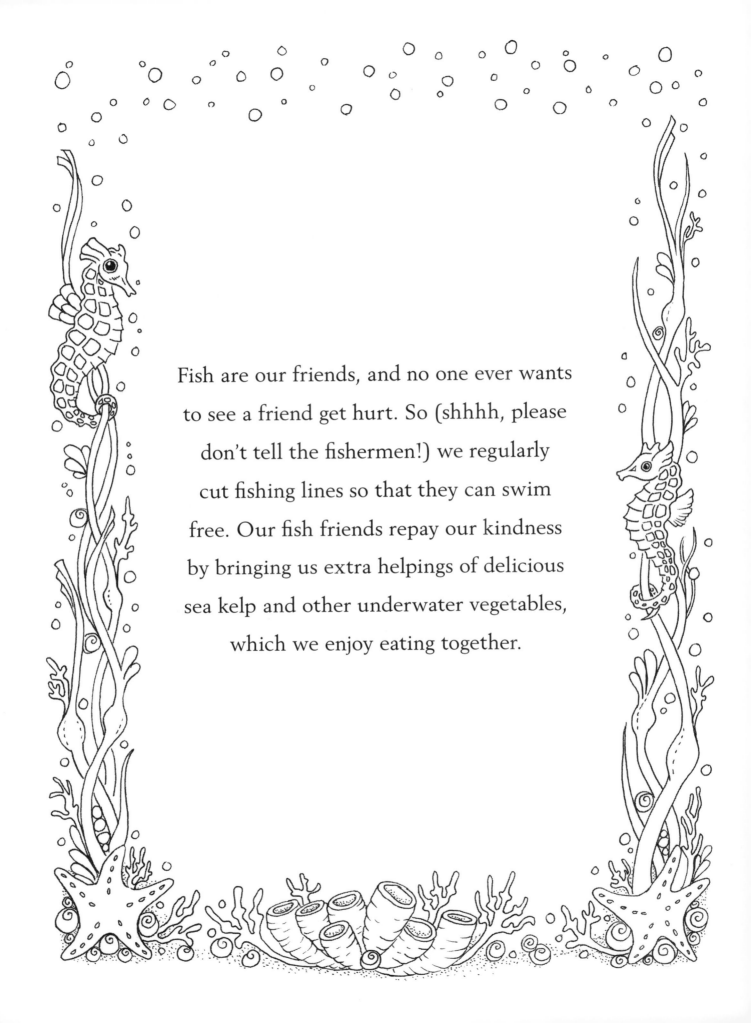

Fish are our friends, and no one ever wants to see a friend get hurt. So (shhhh, please don't tell the fishermen!) we regularly cut fishing lines so that they can swim free. Our fish friends repay our kindness by bringing us extra helpings of delicious sea kelp and other underwater vegetables, which we enjoy eating together.

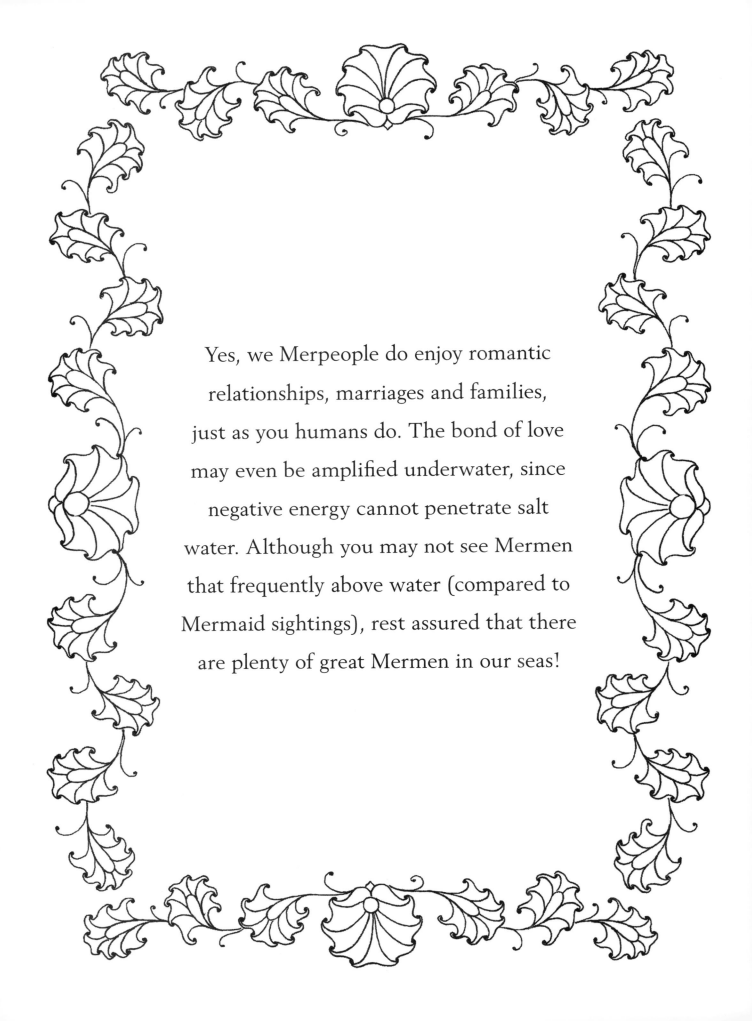

Yes, we Merpeople do enjoy romantic relationships, marriages and families, just as you humans do. The bond of love may even be amplified underwater, since negative energy cannot penetrate salt water. Although you may not see Mermen that frequently above water (compared to Mermaid sightings), rest assured that there are plenty of great Mermen in our seas!

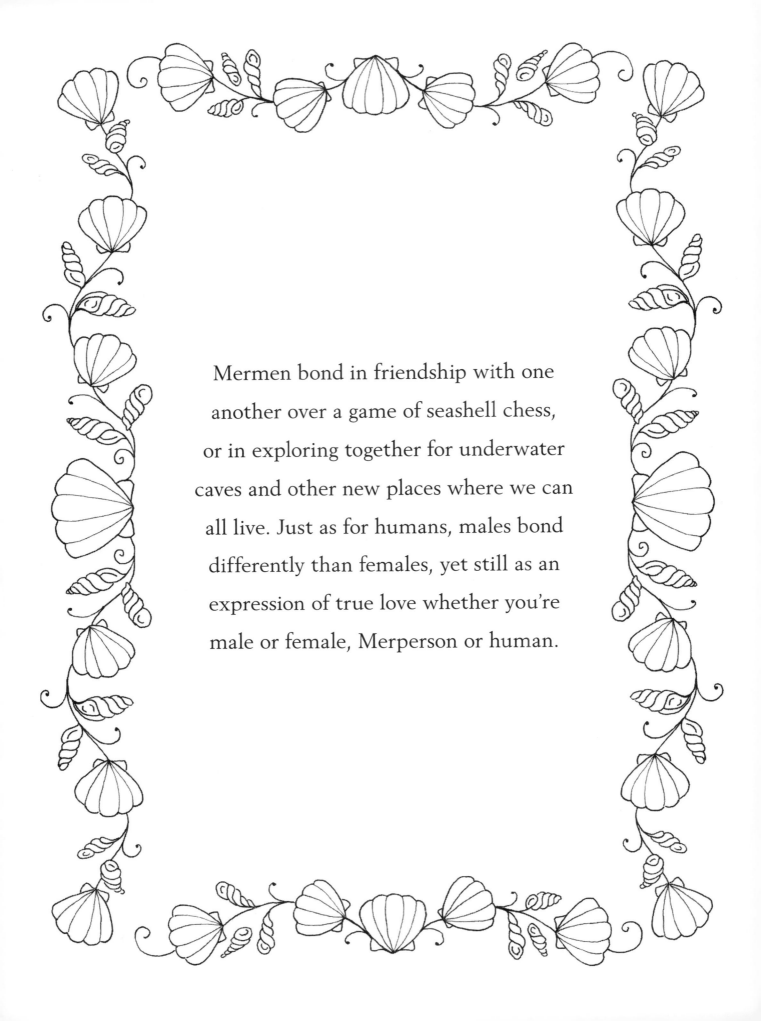

Mermen bond in friendship with one
another over a game of seashell chess,
or in exploring together for underwater
caves and other new places where we can
all live. Just as for humans, males bond
differently than females, yet still as an
expression of true love whether you're
male or female, Merperson or human.

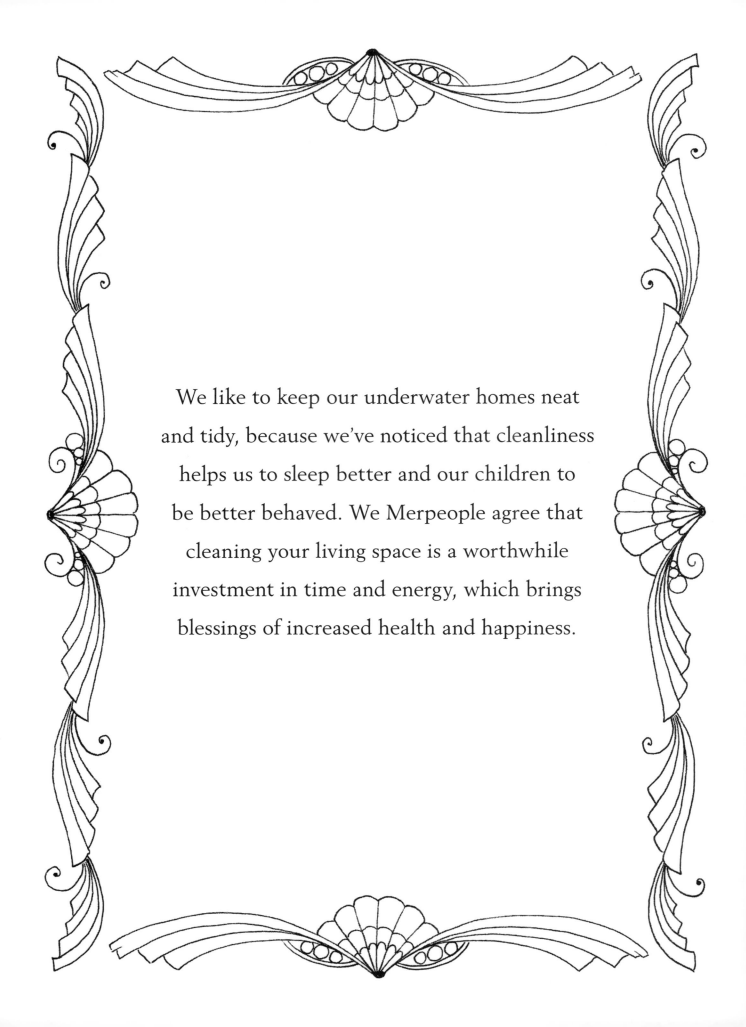

We like to keep our underwater homes neat and tidy, because we've noticed that cleanliness helps us to sleep better and our children to be better behaved. We Merpeople agree that cleaning your living space is a worthwhile investment in time and energy, which brings blessings of increased health and happiness.

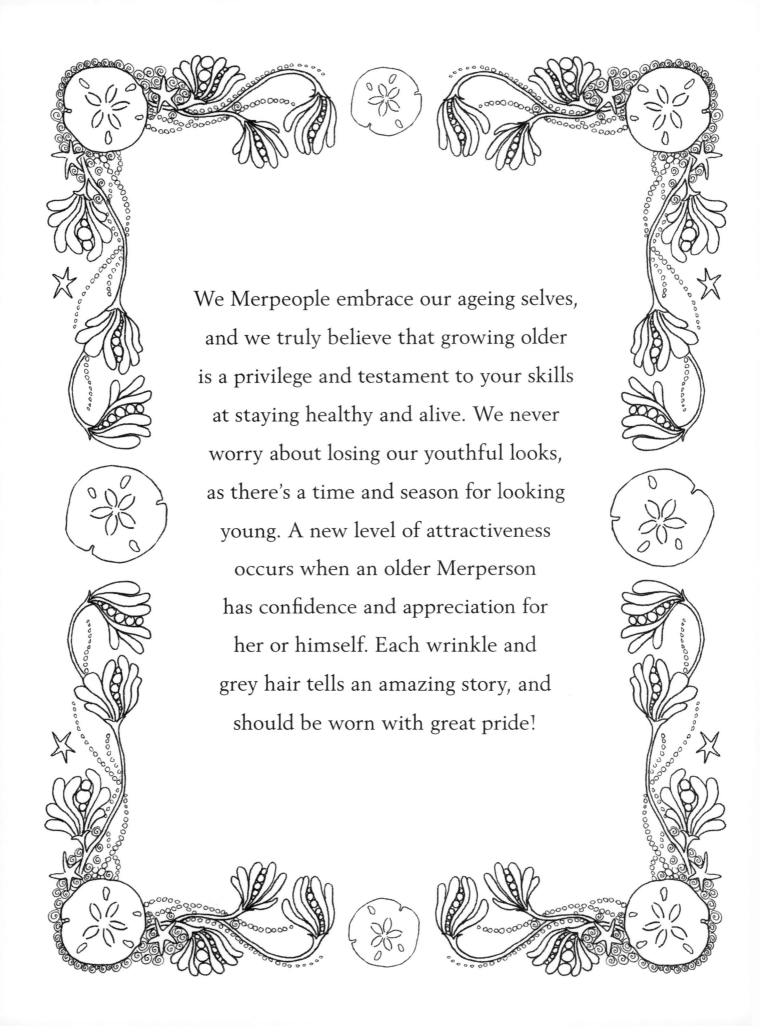

We Merpeople embrace our ageing selves, and we truly believe that growing older is a privilege and testament to your skills at staying healthy and alive. We never worry about losing our youthful looks, as there's a time and season for looking young. A new level of attractiveness occurs when an older Merperson has confidence and appreciation for her or himself. Each wrinkle and grey hair tells an amazing story, and should be worn with great pride!

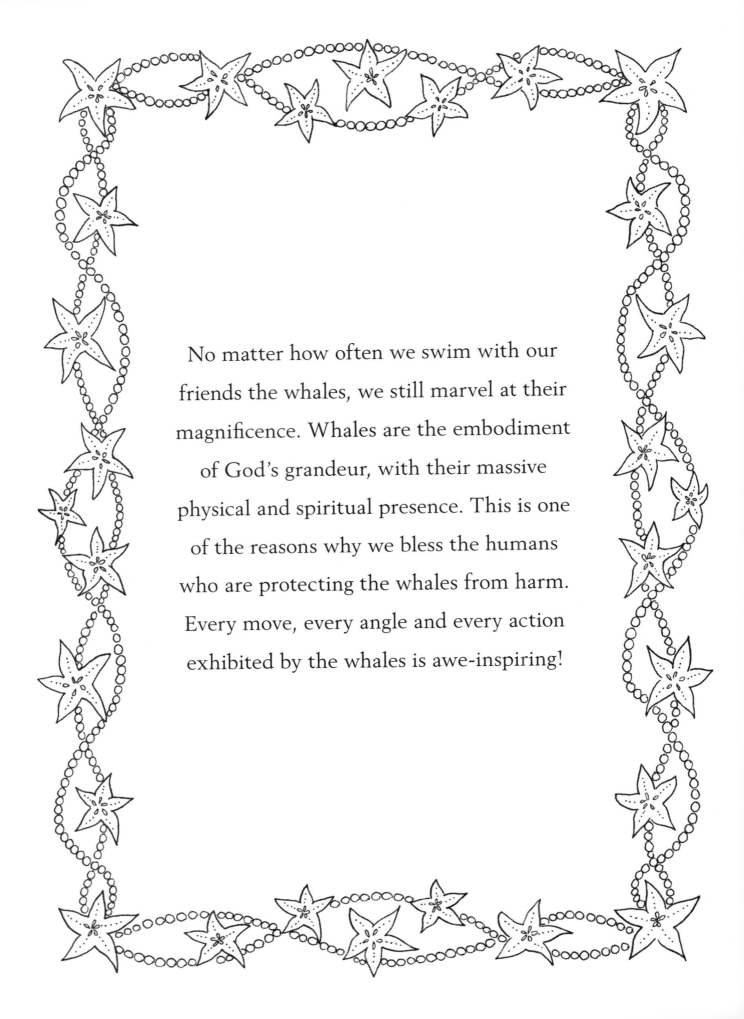

No matter how often we swim with our friends the whales, we still marvel at their magnificence. Whales are the embodiment of God's grandeur, with their massive physical and spiritual presence. This is one of the reasons why we bless the humans who are protecting the whales from harm. Every move, every angle and every action exhibited by the whales is awe-inspiring!

We all have a need for rest, especially
when we're going through life changes.
Resting can help your mind to connect
with God's guidance, to receive divinely
guided ideas for your next passage.
Taking a nap is often one of the most
responsible actions you can do, for it
helps you to step away from worries and
enter into the realm of limitlessness.

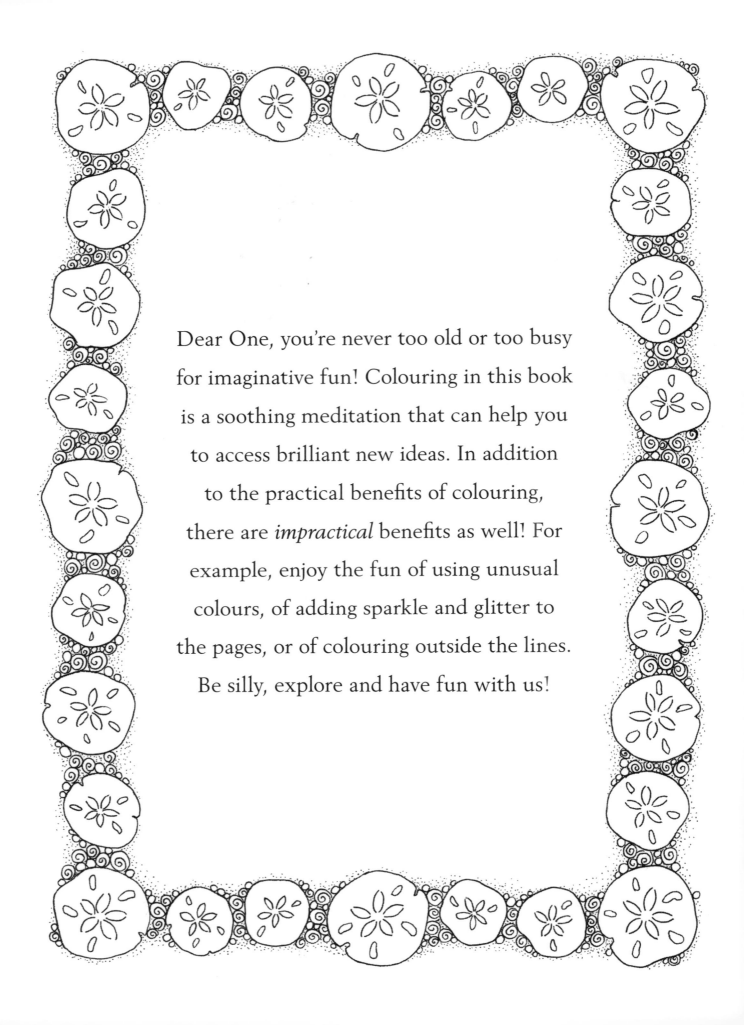

Dear One, you're never too old or too busy for imaginative fun! Colouring in this book is a soothing meditation that can help you to access brilliant new ideas. In addition to the practical benefits of colouring, there are *impractical* benefits as well! For example, enjoy the fun of using unusual colours, of adding sparkle and glitter to the pages, or of colouring outside the lines. Be silly, explore and have fun with us!

We all get upset at times, and that's when having a good friend to talk with can make a positive difference. True friends share equally in talking and listening, and care about the other person's feelings. If you're fortunate enough to have a true friend, please send her or him a hug right now. You can meet a true friend by going to places where others share your interests, such as classes, clubs and groups.

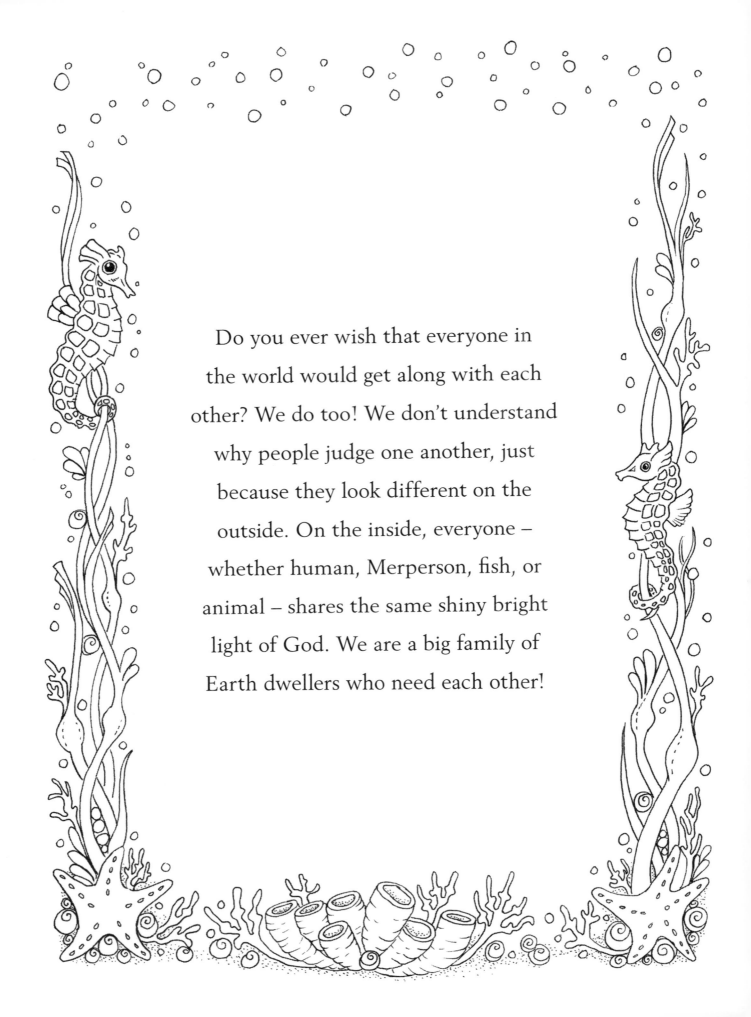

Do you ever wish that everyone in the world would get along with each other? We do too! We don't understand why people judge one another, just because they look different on the outside. On the inside, everyone – whether human, Merperson, fish, or animal – shares the same shiny bright light of God. We are a big family of Earth dwellers who need each other!

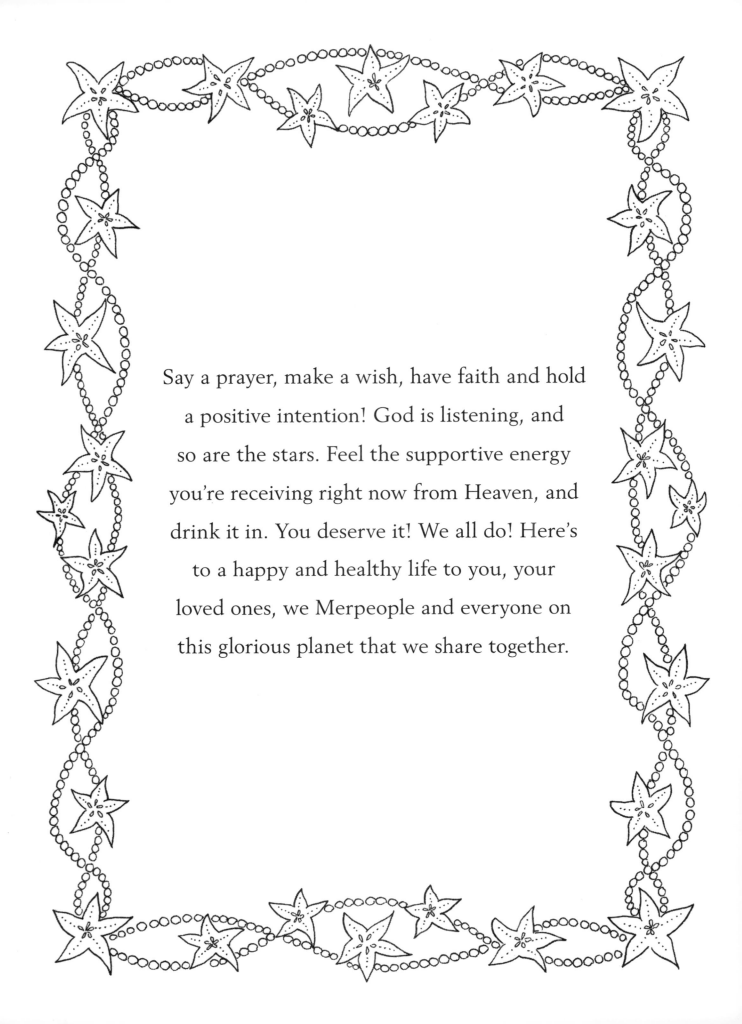

Say a prayer, make a wish, have faith and hold a positive intention! God is listening, and so are the stars. Feel the supportive energy you're receiving right now from Heaven, and drink it in. You deserve it! We all do! Here's to a happy and healthy life to you, your loved ones, we Merpeople and everyone on this glorious planet that we share together.

About the Author

Doreen Virtue holds BA, MA and PhD degrees in counselling psychology. She's the author of more than 50 books and oracle card decks dealing with spiritual topics. Best known for her work with the angels, Doreen is frequently called 'The Angel Lady'.

A lifelong activist and a vegan since 1996, Doreen is involved in charities and movements that support a healthy environment, fair treatment of animals, clean air and water, and organic non-GMO food for all.

Doreen has appeared on *Oprah*, CNN and other television and radio programmes, and writes the weekly column 'My Guardian Angel' for *Woman's World* magazine. Her products are available in most languages worldwide, on Kindle and other eBook platforms and as iTunes apps. She also has a live weekly radio show on Hay House Radio.

www.angeltherapy.com

About the Illustrator

Norma J. Burnell, certified Zentangle® teacher, is an accomplished artist and has been involved in the arts all of her life. She is a contributing author to *The Art of Zentangle* and to *The Art of Fashion Tangling*.

After discovering the art of Zentangle, Norma began incorporating 'tangles' into her own fantasy art and Fairy-Tangles™ was born. Many of her Fairy-Tangles drawings are now sold as rubber stamps for card making and other crafts, and her originals have been sold to collectors around the world.

Norma currently works for a small company creating websites and graphic design. She also teaches various art classes and continues to develop her own art. Her lifelong dream is to continue being an artist and to share her art with others.

www.fairy-tangles.com

Bonus Content

Thank you for purchasing *Messages from the Mermaids Colouring Book* by Doreen Virtue. This product includes a free download! To access this bonus content, please visit www.hayhouse.com/download and enter the Product ID and Download Code as they appear below:

Product ID: 4062

Download Code: book

For further assistance, please contact Hay House Customer Care by phone: US (800) 654-5126 or INTL CC+(760) 431-7695 or visit www.hayhouse.com/contact.

Thank you again for your Hay House purchase. Enjoy!

Hay House, Inc. • P.O. Box 5100 • Carlsbad, CA 92018 • (800) 654-5126

Caution: This audio programme features meditation/visualization exercises that render it inappropriate for use while driving or operating heavy machinery.

Publisher's note: Hay House products are intended to be powerful, inspirational and life-changing tools for personal growth and healing. They are not intended as a substitute for medical care. Please use this audio programme under the supervision of your care provider. Neither the author nor Hay House, Inc., assumes any responsibility for your improper use of this product.

Hay House Colouring Books

9781781807453
£9.99

9781781807460
£9.99

9781781808153
£9.99

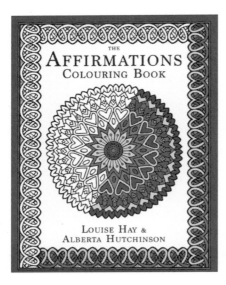

9781781806456
£9.99

9781781807880
£9.99

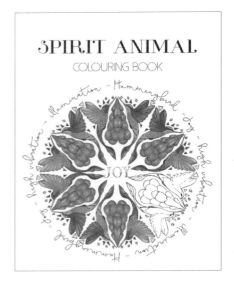

9781781808320
£9.99

www.hayhouse.co.uk

Hay House UK

@HayHouseUK

@hayhouseuk